SEVERE WEATHER

BLIZZARDS

BY SHARON DALGLEISH

Apex is distributed by North Star Editions:
sales@northstareditions.com | 888-417-0195

Produced for Apex by Red Line Editorial.

Photographs ©: Francois Xavier Marit/AFP/Getty Images, cover; Shutterstock Images, 1, 4–5, 9, 13, 14–15, 16–17, 29; iStockphoto, 6–7, 10–11, 12, 20–21, 22–23, 26, 26–27; AP Images, 18; Richard Levine/Alamy, 24–25

Library of Congress Control Number: 2022901433

ISBN
978-1-63738-300-1 (hardcover)
978-1-63738-336-0 (paperback)
978-1-63738-405-3 (ebook pdf)
978-1-63738-372-8 (hosted ebook)

Printed in the United States of America
Mankato, MN
082022

NOTE TO PARENTS AND EDUCATORS

Apex books are designed to build literacy skills in striving readers. Exciting, high-interest content attracts and holds readers' attention. The text is carefully leveled to allow students to achieve success quickly. Additional features, such as bolded glossary words for difficult terms, help build comprehension.

TABLE OF CONTENTS

CHAPTER 1

WHITEOUT

Wind blows snow everywhere. People cannot see the ground or the sky. Everything is blinding white.

In some blizzards, people can't see anything that is more than a few feet away.

A woman is lost outside. She tries to walk in the wind and snow. But the ground is icy. The woman staggers and then falls.

FAST FACT

Some blizzards last a few hours. Others last for days.

During a blizzard, roads often become icy. People can slip and fall.

The woman gets up and keeps walking. Finally, she finds her house. She goes inside. The woman feels lucky. She could have gotten hurt in the storm.

KILLER COLD

Being outside in a blizzard is dangerous. The windchill can freeze bare skin in minutes. People's fingers or toes could freeze, too. Or people can die from hypothermia.

Snow from blizzards can build piles more than 20 feet (6 m) high.

CHAPTER 2

BECOMING A BLIZZARD

A blizzard is a type of snowstorm. But not all snowstorms are blizzards. A blizzard has fast winds. They must go 35 miles per hour (56 km/h).

In some blizzards, winds blow more than 100 miles per hour (161 km/h).

A blizzard's blowing snow can make driving very dangerous.

Some blizzards form when snow is falling. For others, snow is already on the ground. The wind blows lots of snow around. People can't see more than 0.25 miles (0.4 km) away.

Blizzards are more likely to happen in places that are flat.

FAST FACT

In a ground blizzard, the wind picks up snow that has already fallen.

Large blizzards can bring several feet of snow.

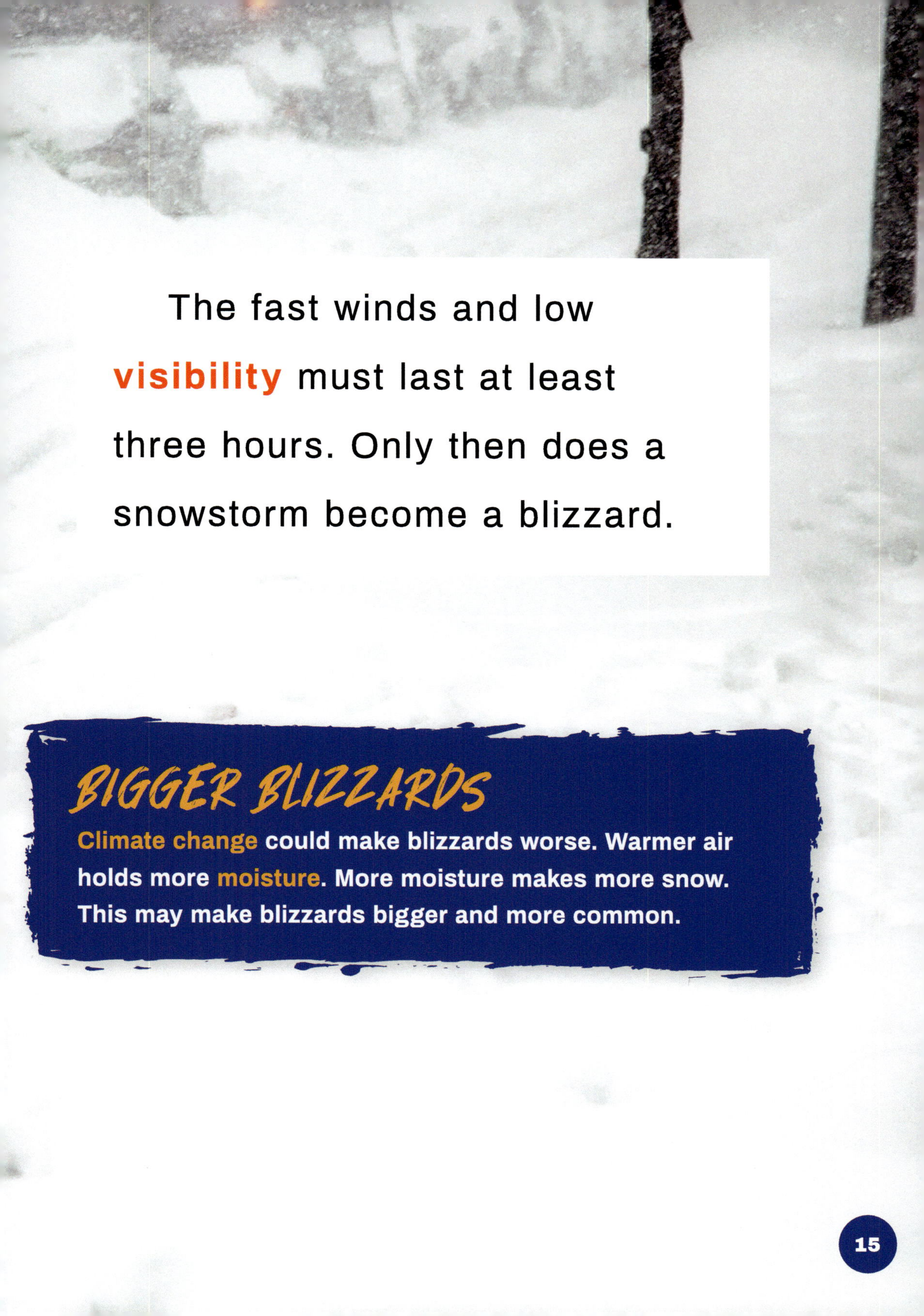

The fast winds and low **visibility** must last at least three hours. Only then does a snowstorm become a blizzard.

BIGGER BLIZZARDS

Climate change could make blizzards worse. Warmer air holds more **moisture**. More moisture makes more snow. This may make blizzards bigger and more common.

CHAPTER 3

RECORD STORMS

In 2016, a blizzard hit the eastern United States. It lasted nine days. More than 630,000 people lost power. The storm was called Snowzilla.

During the Snowzilla blizzard in 2016, some people used skis to get around.

A deadly blizzard hit Iran in 1972. It lasted five days. More than 200 small towns were buried in snow. More than 4,000 people died.

FAST FACT

Iran's 1972 blizzard covered some places in 26 feet (8 m) of snow.

Deep snow trapped many people during the 1972 Iran blizzard.

The Great Blizzard of 1993 was the largest blizzard in history. It spread from Canada to Central America.

After a blizzard, some people must dig their cars out from under the snow.

WHY THE NAME?

Before the 1870s, the word *blizzard* wasn't used for storms. Instead, it meant a cannon shot. Like storms, cannons cause damage. And they make smoke that is hard to see through.

CHAPTER 4

STAYING SAFE

Blizzards cause many problems. Winds bring down power lines and cause **outages**. Snow can block roads. People may become trapped in their homes.

Fast wind or heavy snow can break trees in half.

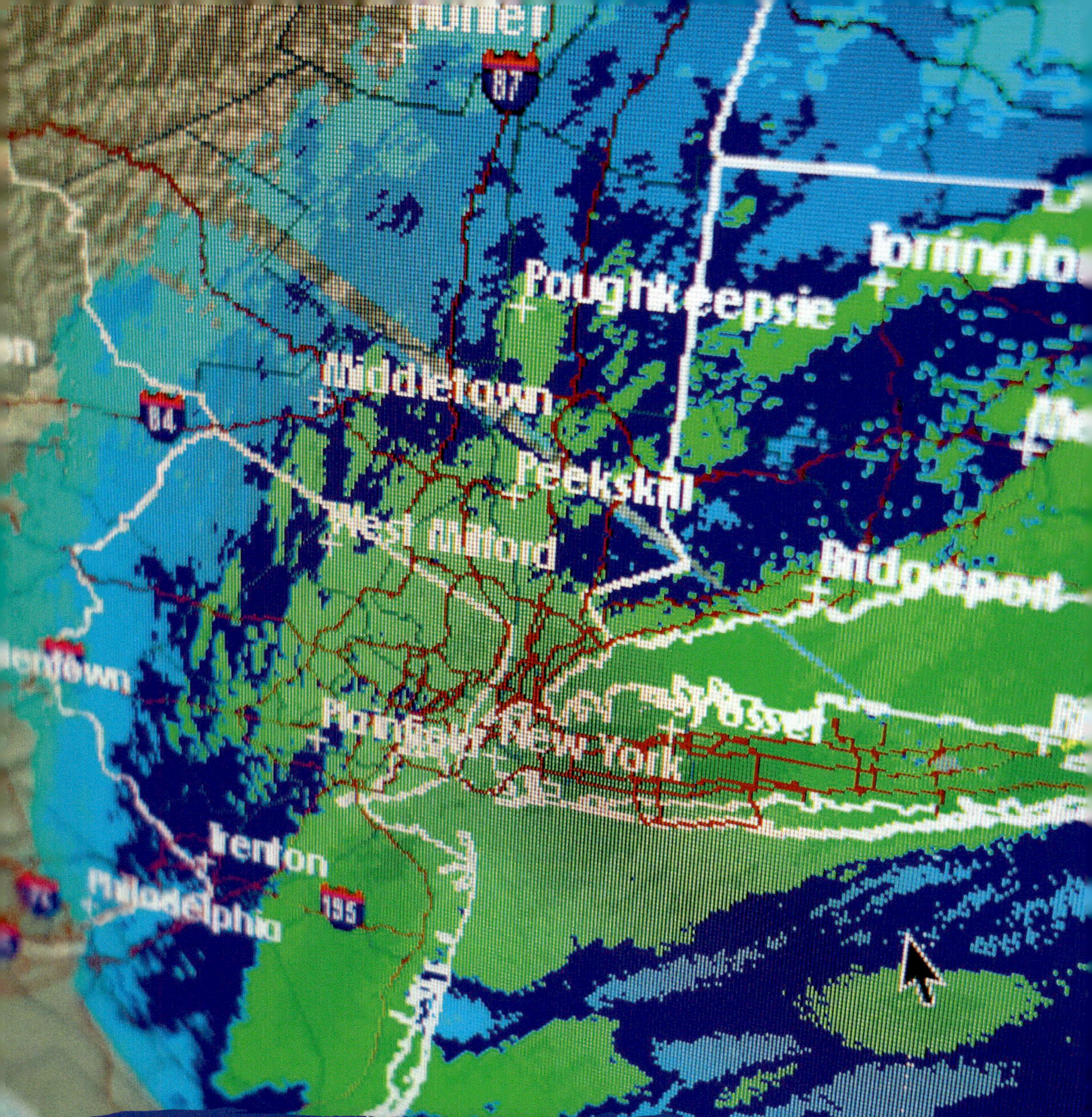

1888 BLIZZARD

A large blizzard hit New York City in 1888. It shut down the whole city. After that, the city built a subway. That way, people could travel underground.

Radar shows scientists where snow is and where wind is moving.

Scientists try to **predict** when a blizzard will hit. They use **radar**. This tool tracks the storm's speed and size. Scientists can warn people in its path.

People often stock up on canned foods before a big storm.

People get warnings on their radios, TVs, or phones. They learn when the storm will hit and how much snow it may bring. They have time to prepare.

Snowplows help keep roads safe during and after blizzards.

FAST FACT

Some blizzards can cause people to lose power for days.

COMPREHENSION QUESTIONS

Write your answers on a separate piece of paper.

1. Write a few sentences describing how blizzards form.

2. Would you like to work as a scientist who studies weather? Why or why not?

3. How long must a snowstorm last to be a blizzard?

- **A.** just a few minutes
- **B.** three hours
- **C.** five days

4. Why would having more snow make blizzards worse?

- **A.** More snow would make the wind slower.
- **B.** More snow would make the air drier.
- **C.** More snow could blow into the air, making it harder to see.

5. What does **blinding** mean in this book?

People cannot see the ground or the sky. Everything is blinding white.

A. moving very fast
B. making things hard to see
C. taking a long time

6. What does **staggers** mean in this book?

But the ground is icy. The woman staggers and then falls.

A. floats in the water
B. walks smoothly and easily
C. takes unsteady steps

Answer key on page 32.

GLOSSARY

climate change

A dangerous long-term change in Earth's temperature and weather patterns.

hypothermia

When a person's body temperature drops dangerously low.

moisture

Water in very small drops.

outages

Losses of electric power.

predict

To say what will happen in the future.

radar

A system that uses radio waves to find the position or speed of something.

visibility

How well and how far people can see.

windchill

A measure of how cold people feel when wind and low temperatures combine.

TO LEARN MORE

BOOKS

Abdo, Kenny. *How to Survive a Blizzard*. Minneapolis: Abdo Publishing, 2019.

London, Martha. *Blizzards*. Minneapolis: Abdo Publishing, 2020.

Rathburn, Betsy. *Blizzards*. Minneapolis: Bellwether Media, 2020.

ONLINE RESOURCES

Visit **www.apexeditions.com** to find links and resources related to this title.

ABOUT THE AUTHOR

Sharon Dalgleish once went for a walk in the snow and sank up to her waist. Luckily, it was not during a blizzard. She now lives in Sydney, Australia, where it never snows.

INDEX

ANSWER KEY:
1. Answers will vary; 2. Answers will vary; 3. B; 4. C; 5. B; 6. C